Welcome

A big hello and a very warm welcome to this huge celebration of Minecraft!

Over the coming pages, we're going to be showcasing some of the very best build projects we've discovered around the world for our favorite video game. We'll also explain some of the brilliant nuances of those builds, and where to find out more about them, too—and hopefully this'll give you loads of ideas for your projects as well!

Ready to get Minecrafting . . . ?!

CONTENTS

FANTASTIC WORLDS

Be inspired by these amazing builds to let your imagination run wild

THEMED BUILDS

Why not pick a fun theme for your custom Minecraft world?

50
XMAS SPIRIT

6
SWORD ISLAND

REAL LIFE

See real places and structures re-created in meticulous detail

28
STATUE OF LIBERTY

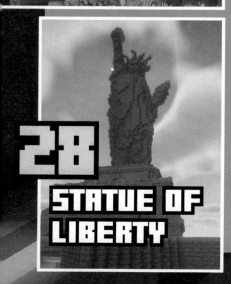

68
ENGLISH COUNTRY HOUSE

SURVIVAL & ADVENTURE MAPS

If you like a good challenge, these worlds are for you

GAMES & MOVIES

Live as your heroes in these big- and small-screen re-creations

REDSTONE GAMES

There's so much fun to be had playing with redstone

Fantastic Worlds

IMAGE: CLOSEEDBR

CREATED BY:
CloseeDBr
DOWNLOAD LINK:
tinyurl.com/mc-swordisland

This amazing build is based on a completely unique idea: an island with a giant stone sword stuck in it. Who knows where it came from or how it got there? In the shade of two giant, custom-built trees, you'll find some small structures and a pathway up the mountain—but what's really going on here remains a mystery. The only other person around is the sailor who got you here, and they're saying nothing! Explore it, expand it, create a story around it—whatever you choose, you'll have a lot of fun on Sword Island.

IMAGE: CLOSEEDBR

IMAGE: CLOSEEDBR

Sword

IMAGE: CLOSEEDBR

DON'T MISS

» **The stone structures and bridges** that tell you you're not the first person here by a long shot . . .

» **The mushroom blocks** used as unconventional decoration alongside other vegetation.

» **Stone and wooden buttons** used to add detailing to other constructions.

IMAGE: CLOSEEDBR

IMAGE: CLOSEEDBR

COOL STUFF

» **The green plants** wrapped around the mountain—are those supposed to be vines?!

» **The villager** in a boat who brought you here—the only other person brave enough to come near Sword Island!

» **A jetty** where boats arriving at and leaving the island can moor.

IMAGE: CLOSEEDBR

Island

Sphen

IMAGE: BALKON

CREATED BY: Balkon
DOWNLOAD LINK:
tinyurl.com/mc-sphen

An expansive map set in a large natural bay, Sphen Keep is filled with secrets and areas to explore. Helpfully, the builder starts you off next to a large map of the area so that you can find your way around, which is useful given the sheer amount of stuff crammed in! Peek in and out of every nook and cranny, and you'll find yourself rewarded for exploring over and over again. Pick up armor, potions, and other items as you go, then imagine just what sort of civilization would have built this strange and exciting place!

IMAGE: BALKON

IMAGE: BALKON

Keep

IMAGE: BALKON

DON'T MISS
» **Several ships** of differing sizes moored in and around the bay.
» **Stuff everywhere**, from item frames packed with goodies like potions and weapons, to armor stands so you can kit yourself out.
» **The buildings and structures** around the rim of the bay—you CAN reach them without cheating . . . !

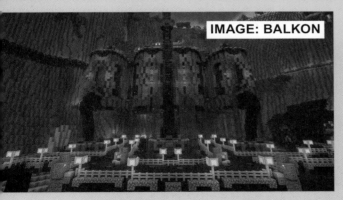
IMAGE: BALKON

IMAGE: BALKON

COOL STUFF
» **Guard towers** and lookout posts so that you can climb the cliffs in safety for a better view.
» **A strange bell tower** that might serve to warn inhabitants of attacks, raids, or other incoming dangers.
» **Beautiful-looking trees** growing out of the cliff faces.

IMAGE: BALKON

IMAGE: WHLDTITAN

Imagined as the capital of the Endermen's world, this Lost End City is like a regular End city, only MUCH bigger and better. An impressive spherical design conceals an End-like landscape filled with buildings to explore, with the whole thing surrounded by a concentric ring, allowing you to view it from any angle. Take care to read the signs carefully in the starting room so that you understand everything you can about the build, then teleport in and prepare to be impressed. Don't worry, though: there are no dragons here—at least, for the moment!

IMAGE: WHLDTITAN

IMAGE: WHLDTITAN

The Lost

IMAGE: WHLDTITAN

DON'T MISS

» **The giant Enderman faces** staring down at you from the central tower.

» **A hidden dropper** that sends you tumbling toward a portal—but what's through it?

» **The outer ring,** which gives you a good view of the city from afar—and can teleport you to the rest of the End.

IMAGE: WHLDTITAN

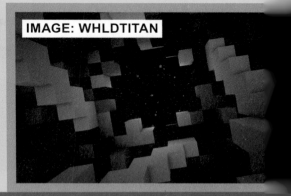

IMAGE: WHLDTITAN

COOL STUFF

» **The symmetrical buildings** echo the design of a normal End city.

» **A huge transparent dome** around the whole city, proving you CAN do curves in Minecraft.

» **End rods and beacons** provide a low level of lighting that illuminates the city beautifully.

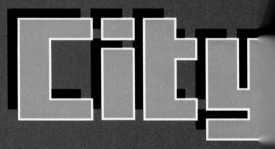

IMAGE: WHLDTITAN

End City

Medieval Village

IMAGE: XEM VAN KAATHOVEN

IMAGE: XEM VAN KAATHOVEN

CREATED BY:
Xem van kaathoven

DOWNLOAD LINK:
tinyurl.com/mc-mountainvillage

Built atop a rocky, mountainous island, this map contains everything you need for a village to thrive, from windmills and farms to a large port where boats can land—even a beach to relax on while you luxuriate in the protection of the castle and its armies. There's so much to explore and surprises to be found everywhere, whether you're peeking your head into one of the small cottages or farmhouses, or getting lost in the castle or cathedral. A great one to explore with friends or on your own.

IMAGE: XEM VAN KAATHOVEN

Mountain

IMAGE: XEM VAN KAATHOVEN

DON'T MISS

» **The amazing dragon statue** that towers above the entire village—is it the Ender dragon, or some kind of rival designed to scare it off?

» **Farms** that will give you the food you need to survive in this map long-term.

» **An End portal** hidden deep within the build. Can you find it on your own?

IMAGE: XEM VAN KAATHOVEN

IMAGE: XEM VAN KAATHOVEN

COOL STUFF

» **A Viking longboat**, come to visit the town and its inhabitants, no doubt bringing treasures from afar.

» **A huge keep on the mountaintop**, facing out to sea, which you can reach on foot.

» **A sorcerer's tower**, with a spell-casting station at the top and fires that burn forever.

IMAGE: XEM VAN KAATHOVEN

IMAGE: MADDEN

CREATED BY:
Madden
DOWNLOAD LINK:
tinyurl.com/mc-fishermanslake

This small but beautiful map imagines a fisherman's lake, secluded in a natural mountain bay, the sides of which are lined with flowers and greenery. Within the bay are several fishing boats, moored for shelter and connected by pathways of lily pads—hope you enjoy a jumping puzzle! There may not be much to explore, but you'll catch some amazing views and it's a fun map for playing hide-and-seek with friends or just wandering around and taking in the relaxing nature of it.

IMAGE: MADDEN

IMAGE: MADDEN

The Fisherm

IMAGE: MADDEN

DON'T MISS

» **The cargo-laden** holds in the ships, where you can stock up on items.
» **The waterfalls** cascading down the sides of the lake, which you can swim up if you dare!
» **A jetty** attached to one of the ships, leading to a small patch of land on which to rest.

IMAGE: MADDEN

IMAGE: MADDEN

COOL STUFF

» **Three fishing boats** filled with different features to spend time exploring.
» **A large floating island** pours water down into the lake below from up high.
» **Deep, clear waters** in the style of a calming lagoon.

IMAGE: MADDEN

an's Lake

Cloud Sky

Ever wished you could live up among the clouds? With Cloud Sky, you can! This small but beautifully formed build replaces the entire world with a few clouds, constructed from a combination of white glass, white concrete powder, and light-emitting blocks to create a world you could imagine existing high above the Overworld. What's more, nestled in the largest cloud is a house inside a crescent moon, with multiple floors and some ornate detailing. It's not quite a stop in heaven, but it's the closest Minecraft can get right now!

IMAGE: MADALYNNALINE

IMAGE: MADALYNNALINE

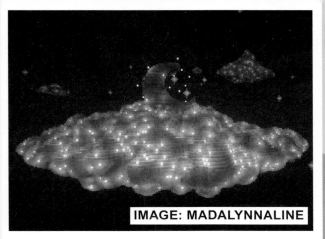

IMAGE: MADALYNNALINE

IMAGE: MADALYNNALINE

IMAGE: MADALYNNALINE

DON'T MISS

» **The entrance to the house** at the bottom, just where the moon sits atop the clouds.

» **The plant-filled library**, where you could relax for hours in peaceful contemplation.

» **The sight of the entire build** at night, when it shimmers magnificently.

IMAGE: MADALYNNALINE

IMAGE: MADALYNNALINE

COOL STUFF

» **The spiral staircase** that winds its way from the top to the bottom of the moon house.

» **The book and quills** laid on the desk using item frames.

» **Tables made of trapdoors**—a furniture idea you can reuse yourself!

CREATED BY:
Zeemo
DOWNLOAD LINK:
tinyurl.com/mc-worldofworlds

Re-creating a city or a landmark in Minecraft is one thing, but this builder has done something extraordinary and crammed in almost 100 different locations into the "World of Worlds"—explore this ginormous map and find re-creations of buildings from across the globe. From London to Las Vegas, from Moscow to Milan, from Beijing to Buenos Aires, you can visit all sorts of familiar sights right next to one another. Best of all, every building is fully rendered with detailed interiors. See the globe without leaving your armchair—a world so big you'll never want to leave.

IMAGE: ZEEMO

IMAGE: ZEEMO

IMAGE: ZEEMO

World of

IMAGE: ZEEMO

DON'T MISS

» **The colossal palace of Versailles**—so big we could barely fit it into one screenshot.
» **The Las Vegas section**—not just a building, but a whole section of the famous strip.
» **Updates to the map**, released constantly with new additions (we saw version 3.7).

IMAGE: ZEEMO

IMAGE: ZEEMO

IMAGE: ZEEMO

COOL STUFF

» More than just **single buildings** next to each other, World of Worlds is its own huge city.
» **Vehicles** have been added to the world to make it even more realistic.
» **A canal system and waterway** that you can use to traverse the world if you like!

Worlds

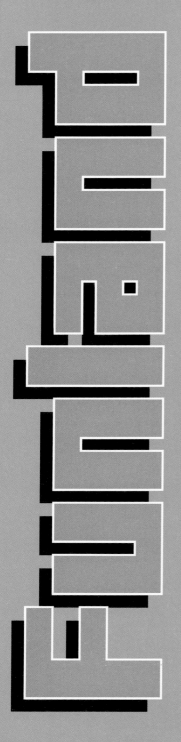

Funland

CREATED BY:
Superpish

DOWNLOAD LINK: tinyurl.com/mc-funland

Haven't we all dreamed of controlling our own theme park? This map, christened Funland 3, gives us the chance to finally do that—in Minecraft, at least. Fingers crossed you're not creeped out by clowns, because there are tons around this crazily dense wonderland, alongside roller coasters and other attractions, all designed to make Minecraft as fun as a day out. Whether you enjoy the experience with friends or stage your own theme-park zombie apocalypse is up to you, but we're sure that however you end up playing in the map, you'll have a great time doing it. And hey, it's cheaper than a family ticket!

IMAGE: SUPERPISH

IMAGE: SUPERPISH

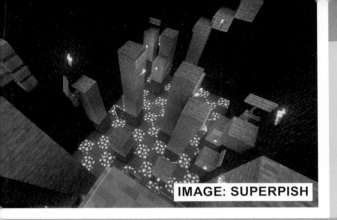

IMAGE: SUPERPISH

DON'T MISS

» **A fully designed parkour** jumping puzzle for you to complete—if you're good enough.

» **The roller coaster** where you take a plunge through a flaming hoop while off the rails.

» **An awesome lighthouse/helter-skelter** to climb.

IMAGE: SUPERPISH

IMAGE: SUPERPISH

COOL STUFF

» **A giant Enderman** towering above the map with a box in his outstretched arms.

» **Pixel art** everywhere, enhancing the fun of just looking around, whether you ride anything or not!

» **Crazy drops, jumps, and falls** that you can easily survive—if you don't lose your nerve . . .

IMAGE: SUPERPISH

IMAGE: SUPERPISH

CREATED BY: THEJESTR

DOWNLOAD LINK: tinyurl.com/mc-greenfield

Built over the course of 10 (yes, 10!) years, Greenfield might be the most impressive city we've ever seen in Minecraft. A full-scale creation based loosely on Los Angeles, it's taken the work of 50 people acting together to create a city so detailed you could almost swear it was real. It's so huge we've barely scratched the surface of it in our explorations, but that does mean you'll need a powerful PC to explore it properly! What's more, the makers insist this map is less than half finished. We can't imagine what it'll look like in the future.

IMAGE: THEJESTR

IMAGE: THEJESTR

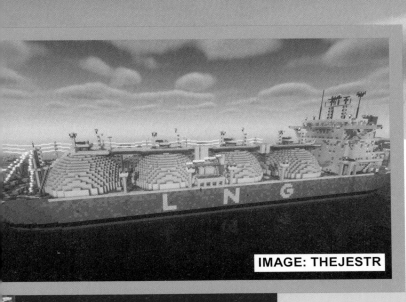

IMAGE: THEJESTR

IMAGE: THEJESTR

COOL STUFF

» **Every building** has its own full-scale interior, packed with details and Easter eggs.

» **Divided into neighborhoods** of different character and appearance, it feels like exploring an actual city.

» **A hub world** that allows you to teleport quickly between parts of the city—thankfully, because it'd take hours to cross on foot!

DON'T MISS

» **The cruise ship** waiting in the docks, complete with lifeboats and shipping features around it.

» **A coal power station** being built—or is it dismantled?—in the industrial part of town.

» **The shopping mall and movie theater** building in Clinton, as perfect an urban space as we've ever seen!

IMAGE: THEJESTR

IMAGE: THEJESTR

Imperi

IMAGE: RIGOLO

CREATED BY: Rigolo
DOWNLOAD LINK:
tinyurl.com/mc-imperialcity

The Imperial City imagines a world where the classical styles of every culture evolved together into an enormous, detailed, and regal city that's more impressive than anything that has ever existed in real life. Ornate exteriors and grand interiors mean every time you enter or leave a building, you're certain to see something impressive. Filled with palaces and temples, plazas and boulevards, it's almost beyond imagination—or it would be if someone hadn't imagined it. It'll take hours to explore, and you'll have a ton of fun doing it.

IMAGE: RIGOLO

IMAGE: RIGOLO

al City

IMAGE: RIGOLO

DON'T MISS

» **The huge skull-faced statues**, which sit at the side of a cliff cradling fire cauldrons.

» The sheer majesty of an **imperial palace** surrounded by canals and waterways.

» **A grand marketplace plaza**, overlooked by an incredible public clock face.

IMAGE: RIGOLO

IMAGE: RIGOLO

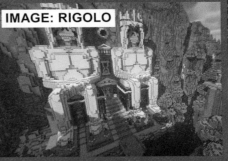

IMAGE: RIGOLO

COOL STUFF

» **So big** you could spend days here without seeing everything.

» **The numerous photo opportunities** created by the intersection of the city and wilderness.

» **The dedication** to keeping the entire city visually similar.

Real
Life

Ever wanted to visit the Statue of Liberty? Well, this is the next best thing—a Minecraft re-creation of the statue and its base. This is a 1:1 replica, meaning every block in the game represents one yard in real life, so you really can get a feel for the statue and its surroundings! It's perfect for editing into your own maps or if you just want to enjoy a historic landmark in Minecraft. Either way, you'll have loads of fun, whether you're building on and around the statue or just admiring it from afar.

IMAGE: SERIOUSCRAFT

IMAGE: SERIOUSCRAFT

IMAGE: SERIOUSCRAFT

Statue of

IMAGE: SERIOUSCRAFT

DON'T MISS

» **The restrooms** on either side of the entrance, with sinks and cubicles to copy for your own builds.

» **The intricate interiors**, lined with gorgeous architectural flourishes.

» **The hidden room** beneath the statue, filled with glowstone to keep the creepers out!

IMAGE: SERIOUSCRAFT

IMAGE: SERIOUSCRAFT

COOL STUFF

» **The statue** is made of copper blocks, so you can watch it turn the iconic green color of the real statue!

» **The star-shaped base** can be entered and explored, just like in real life.

» **The statue** might not look like much up close, but from afar the silhouette is perfect!

IMAGE: SERIOUSCRAFT

Liberty

SS Colossal

DOWNLOAD LINK: tinyurl.com/mc-sscolossal

Ocean liners are popular for Minecraft map builders, but few are as incredible as the SS *Colossal*, which is a truly massive ocean liner inspired by real life. With nine decks in total, the SS *Colossal* was designed to look amazing outside while being feature-complete inside. With not a single piece of interior space unused, there are hundreds of rooms and facilities to explore. A fantastic map for a multiplayer hide-and-seek experience—but, like a real ocean liner, you can have plenty of fun just looking around!

IMAGE: NICKO91

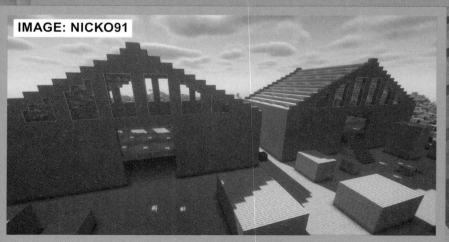

IMAGE: NICKO91

IMAGE: NICKO91

IMAGE: NICKO91

IMAGE: NICKO91

COOL STUFF

» As well as **the ship** itself, you get a dockyard and warehouse area to explore!

» **Actual steam** rising from the chimneys—check it out to see how it's done!

» **Hundreds of cabins** for you and your friends to decorate as your own.

DON'T MISS

» **The bridge deck** and its selection of controls—accessible to captains only, of course.

» **The relaxing lounge area**, with couches and plants, and access to the major facilities such as a café, restaurant, bank, bakery, and much more!

» **An on-deck swimming pool** with diving board, plus skating rinks, a gym, and other sports facilities belowdecks.

IMAGE: NICKO91

IMAGE: NICKO91

Beauty

CREATED BY: Tepleier

DOWNLOAD LINK:
tinyurl.com/mc-beautyvalley

Sometimes all you want out of Minecraft is a completely unspoiled landscape, and there's no landscape so unspoiled as Beauty Valley. There's just a single house in the whole of this huge, mountainous valley filled with beautiful trees and water features. Whether you decide to introduce more civilization here or just enjoy being out in the wilderness, it's a map that's great to explore and is lovingly crafted to look amazing—it looks especially good if you have shaders installed, so break out your favorite and go enjoy the view!

IMAGE: TEPLEIER

IMAGE: TEPLEIER

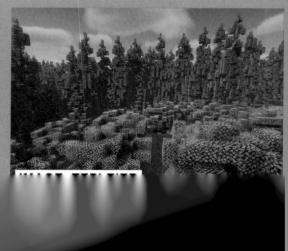

Valley

IMAGE: TEPLEIER

DON'T MISS

» **Your mountain house**, an oasis of modern comfort in the otherwise rugged landscape.

» **The great lake** that makes the landscape even more picturesque and serene.

» **A huge open meadow** in the shadow of a mountain, filled with friendly and peaceful mobs.

IMAGE: TEPLEIER

IMAGE: TEPLEIER

IMAGE: TEPLEIER

COOL STUFF

» **Sheer cliffs and rolling mountains** that Minecraft would never generate by itself.

» **A huge variety of trees**, crafted to look more realistic than ever.

» **Incredible views** from just about any point on the map—take plenty of screenshots!

Golf and Country Club

CREATED BY:
J Sanders
DOWNLOAD LINK:
tinyurl.com/mc-golfclub

Built in two months, this re-creation of a golf and country club is a holiday resort with a twist—an actual game to play! Find the greens and use a bow and arrow to simulate hitting a golf ball. The fewer shots you take to reach the hole, the better your chance of winning. Alongside that fantastic idea, you'll find an incredible, well-manicured estate with multiple buildings, each given their own interior. Whether you enjoy golf or not, you can only imagine how relaxing it'd be to spend time here!

IMAGE: J SANDERS

IMAGE: J SANDERS

IMAGE: J SANDERS

IMAGE: J SANDERS

DON'T MISS

» **The secret spa** area hidden below the mansion, with pools and hot tub areas.
» **The incredible arched interior** of the main country club mansion.
» **The indoor driving range**, where you can practice your shots in a controlled way.

IMAGE: J SANDERS

IMAGE: J SANDERS

COOL STUFF

» **An actual "golf" game** you can play using a bow and arrow, with greens, fairways, and sand traps.
» **Huge grounds**, with horse paddocks and walking/jogging routes so you can enjoy the area peacefully.
» **A fully built country club** with a complete set of interior locations to explore.

IMAGE: J SANDERS

IMAGE: A LEGEND

CREATED BY:
A Legend
DOWNLOAD LINK:
tinyurl.com/mc-luxurious

Everyone has dreamed of building their perfect mansion in Minecraft, and S's Luxurious House is one of the best examples we've ever seen. As well as being supermodern in its design and interiors, it has ornate and well-designed gardens that would make any historic mansion look positively pedestrian. Pity the gardener who has to keep that place in order, but luckily you get to enjoy it without having to do any of the work! Whether you just admire the building or move in and redecorate, *luxurious* is definitely the word this build brings to mind.

IMAGE: A LEGEND

IMAGE: A LEGEND

S's Luxurious

IMAGE: A LEGEND

DON'T MISS

» **The outdoor hot tub** in the garden, perfect for enjoying summer evenings outside.

» The house's very own **massage and meditation room**.

» **The huge fountain** at the end of the driveway—practically hypnotic!

IMAGE: A LEGEND

IMAGE: A LEGEND

COOL STUFF

» **A massive modern house**, created using the most up-to-date interior design ideas.

» **Rooms for all members** of the family, young and old.

» **Impressive decoration** and furniture in every part of the build—no shortcuts here!

IMAGE: A LEGEND

Modern House

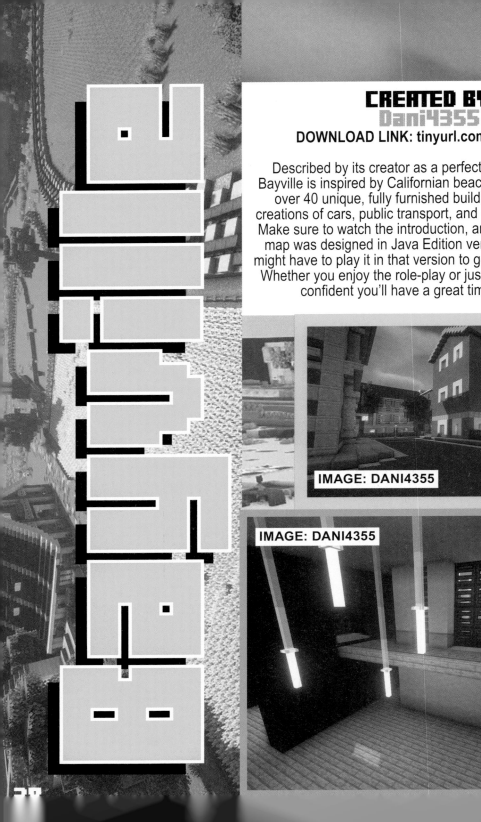

BAYVILLE

CREATED BY:
Dani4355
DOWNLOAD LINK: tinyurl.com/mc-bayville

Described by its creator as a perfect map for role-play, Bayville is inspired by Californian beach cities and contains over 40 unique, fully furnished buildings alongside re-creations of cars, public transport, and other urban features. Make sure to watch the introduction, and be aware that this map was designed in Java Edition version 1.16.5, so you might have to play it in that version to get the full experience. Whether you enjoy the role-play or just go exploring, we're confident you'll have a great time in Bayville!

IMAGE: DANI4355

IMAGE: DANI4355

IMAGE: DANI4355

DON'T MISS

» **A hospital**, complete with red cross above the door and red detailing on the roof.

» **The beach area**, lined with palm trees and sun loungers.

» **A working kelp factory** that you can use to help produce food or earn money in.

IMAGE: DANI4355

IMAGE: DANI4355

COOL STUFF

» **A control room** in the town hall that allows you to turn command block features on and off.

» An in-game **currency of emeralds** that you can spend and acquire.

» **A working train** that'll take you to a neighboring farm village in the countryside.

IMAGE: DANI4355

IMAGE: DANI4355

Osfjoll

IMAGE: ANSON

IMAGE: ANSON

CREATED BY:
Anson
DOWNLOAD LINK:
tinyurl.com/mc-osfjoll

Pronounced "awhs-fall," Osfjoll is a Scandinavian-inspired island city with hospitals, schools, a park, an ice-skating rink, and more. You can even take a hike up to a huge volcano! Best of all, the creator has populated it with "people" using armor stands and character heads. If that's too much for your PC, you can also find a version without them by following the link above and checking out the creator's YouTube channel. You'll have a great time exploring as you get transported to a landscape unlike any other!

IMAGE: ANSON

IMAGE: ANSON

IMAGE: ANSON

DON'T MISS

» **The ice cream parlor** and its selection of flavors.

» **A natural ice rink** populated with skaters.

» **A small cruise ship** at the docks of one of the city districts.

IMAGE: ANSON

IMAGE: ANSON

COOL STUFF

» **Interiors** in every building, with places to relax, explore, or move into!

» **Multiple city districts** with their own layouts, facilities, and populations.

» **A volcano** at the heart of the island—don't worry, it is safe!

IMAGE: ANSON

CREATED BY: SANAR
DOWNLOAD LINK:
tinyurl.com/mc-islandresort

If a vacation is what you're after, this island resort build is the perfect choice. Set on a custom-built island with a huge beach, picturesque mountains, and a smattering of trees surrounding it, you'll find everything you need for some time off right here. Take a dip in the pool, the natural lagoon, or the clear blue sea around it. Climb the mountains or one of the observation towers in the futuristic hotel. Or relax on the beach, in one of the many vacation homes, or your own personal lodgings. Fully equipped in every corner of the build, there's always something to enjoy at the island resort!

IMAGE: SANAR

IMAGE: SANAR

IMAGE: SANAR

Island

IMAGE: SANAR

DON'T MISS

» The fantastic **pool area**, great for relaxing by or having a long swim in.

» The many **food shops**, where you can swap your hard-earned cash for drinks and snacks.

» A **helicopter build** perched on top of one of the hotel's multiple helipads.

IMAGE: SANAR

IMAGE: SANAR

COOL STUFF

» Intricate use of **glass blocks** in constructing a hotel that looks incredible and never feels cramped.

» Carefully designed **pathways and facilities** so that you can get around the resort easily and quickly.

» A full **population of residents** to take your inspiration from, whatever activity you're doing.

IMAGE: SANAR

Resort

CHICAGO

CREATED BY: Luke
DOWNLOAD LINK: tinyurl.com/mc-chicago1

It's hard to build a real city in Minecraft, but this builder has done an incredible job re-creating the look of Chicago, Illinois. Built to 1:4 scale, this map copies the layout and appearance of Chicago, as well as a number of famous landmarks, all in a slightly miniaturized form. Whether you're a resident, a tourist, or someone who has never been there, you can enjoy the famous "Windy City" without ever leaving your home. This is a build packed with unique features, innovative ideas, and a genuine love of the city it is replicating. If you don't love it, we'll eat our hats.

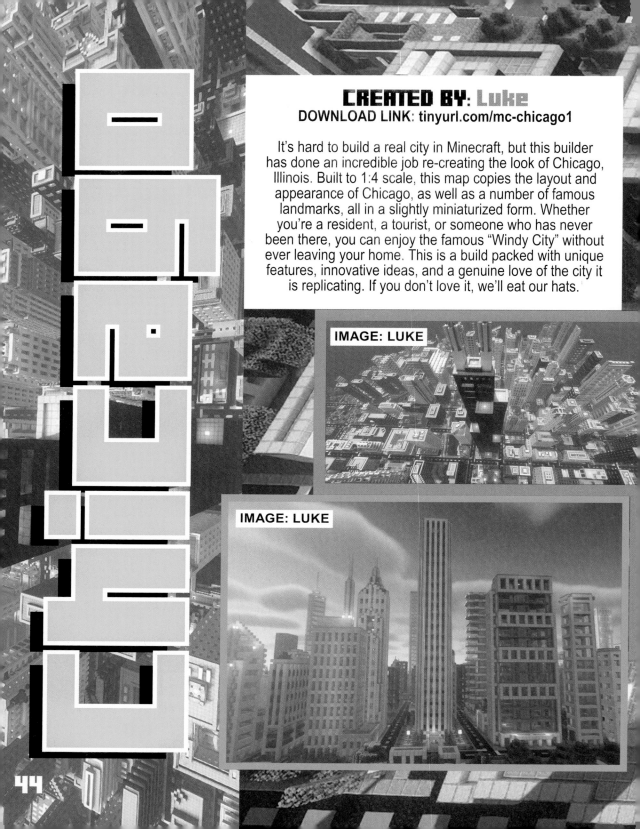

IMAGE: LUKE

IMAGE: LUKE

44

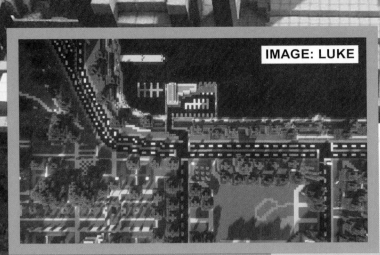

IMAGE: LUKE

IMAGE: LUKE

COOL STUFF

» **A fully connected road system** that you can follow around the city and beyond.

» **Brilliant use of textures** to re-create the look of buildings of all different materials.

» **Massive detail** everywhere, including a number of building interiors to explore.

DON'T MISS

» **The railway system**, which can take you around the city when even flying is too much work.

» **Huge, lovingly crafted parks** with everything from baseball fields to tree-lined boulevards.

» **Massive skyscrapers**, including some of Chicago's most famous towers!

IMAGE: LUKE

IMAGE: LUKE

IMAGE: LUKE

45

Soviet Mos

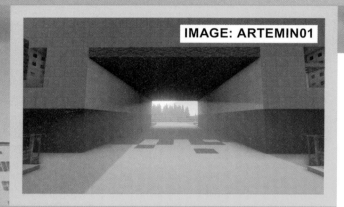

IMAGE: ARTEMIN01

IMAGE: ARTEMIN01

CREATED BY:
artemin01
DOWNLOAD LINK:
tinyurl.com/mc-moscow1963

1960s Russia was a mysterious place that few Westerners visited, so it's up to Minecraft builders to try to re-create what it might have been like. This tiny slice of Soviet Moscow is so desolate that at first it feels like the entire build might be in black and white—but as the sun rises and the weather clears, you see the snow-covered brilliance of the city. With eight fully furnished blocks, the forest, and a farm, this is a great Survival map for playing with friends or a place to have some eerie experiences.

IMAGE: ARTEMIN01

C.O.W.: 1963

IMAGE: ARTEMIN01

DON'T MISS

>> **The streetlights**, which look surprisingly atmospheric in the foggy weather.

>> The re-creations of blocky **1960s cars**—exactly what Minecraft's good for!

>> The **Soviet-era murals** painted on the sides of some buildings—they look better from a few steps back!

IMAGE: ARTEMIN01

IMAGE: ARTEMIN01

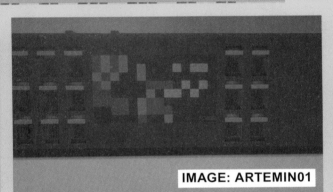

COOL STUFF

>> Accurate re-creations of **Soviet postwar housing blocks**.

>> **Fence posts** used to create **dead trees**—a fantastic idea for your own builds!

>> **Furnished interiors** so that you can move in and experience life in 1960s Russia.

Themed
Builds

IMAGE: MR_KIYE

CREATED BY:
Mr_Kiye
DOWNLOAD LINK:
tinyurl.com/mc-xmasspirit

Just because it's Minecraft doesn't mean you can't celebrate the holidays, and that's exactly what one builder has done with this Christmas-themed Minecraft creation. A small, cozy cabin in some snowy woods is exactly the sort of place to have your perfect Christmas party. Explore every corner to find all the Christmas-themed stuff, from candy cane decorations outdoors to presents indoors and—of course—the tree. It might not be Christmas when you're reading this, but in this world, it can be Christmas every day.

IMAGE: MR_KIYE

IMAGE: MR_KIYE

Xmas

IMAGE: MR_KIYE

DON'T MISS

» **The presents** scattered around the map—actually retextured mob heads!
» **The tiny potted spruce trees** that resemble miniature Christmas trees. Smart move!
» **The secret room** hidden somewhere around the map. It's not too hard to find!

IMAGE: MR_KIYE

IMAGE: MR_KIYE

COOL STUFF

» **Atmospheric lighting** designed to make the whole place look best at night.
» **Heavy theming** of red and green colors, including in the windows.
» **A mixture of Christmassy and wintry ideas**, from snow and log fires to cake and presents.

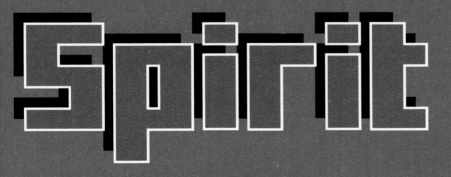

IMAGE: MR_KIYE

Spirit

Victoria

IMAGE: JUMBO STUDIO

CREATED BY:
Jumbo Studio

DOWNLOAD LINK:
tinyurl.com/mc-victorianhouse

If you dream of living in a Victorian-style mansion house, but with all the modern conveniences of today, then this map is the one for you. Its classic exterior hides an up-to-date interior, with everything from a big-screen TV to an ultramodern kitchen. The bathroom is particularly great if you're looking for furniture ideas for your own builds! Outdoors you'll find all sorts of cool additions, including a garden swing and a plant nursery. The grounds are finished off with a garage/gatehouse for additional storage. It's a perfect build to use as the basis for an adventure map or to set up a base in for Survival mode.

IMAGE: JUMBO STUDIO

IMAGE: JUMBO STUDIO

n HOUSE

IMAGE: JUMBO STUDIO

DON'T MISS

» **The hanging baskets** outdoors, incorporating potted plants and chains.
» **The simple garden wall** and bushes on the boundary of the property.
» **Tons of great furniture** ideas that you can put in your own builds.

IMAGE: JUMBO STUDIO

IMAGE: JUMBO STUDIO

COOL STUFF

» **This is a simple build** with only a few different block types—easy to copy and/or remake.
» **A smart but simple design** that'll impress any visitors with its old-style looks.
» **An atmospheric build** that works perfectly with its spruce forest location.

IMAGE: JUMBO STUDIO

IMAGE: PMKEXPERT

IMAGE: PMKEXPERT

CREATED BY:
PmkExpert
DOWNLOAD LINK:
tinyurl.com/mc-summersecrets

This map features a resort and water park named Summer Secrets and was created over the course of seven years! Filled with custom 3D models and interactive objects, it includes playable games, water slides, and a huge number of exciting creations. Check out the natural waves lapping on the shore! The link above will also point you at datapacks that let you add working showers, actual beach volleyball, water slides, and much more! With Easter eggs everywhere and many custom features, this is one map sure to impress everyone who sets foot in it.

IMAGE: PMKEXPERT

Summer

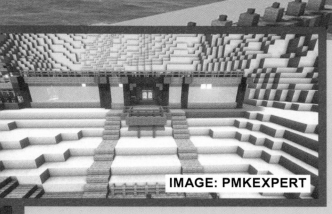

IMAGE: PMKEXPERT

DON'T MISS

» The **secret water caves**, where you can see out the side of a mountain for amazing views.

» The **surprisingly detailed 3D models** that have been added into the game using a resource pack.

» A **beach shop** with custom items available for purchase.

IMAGE: PMKEXPERT

IMAGE: PMKEXPERT

COOL STUFF

» **A huge desert location** transformed into an oasis of fun and relaxation.

» **A boating lake** with a predefined path, so you can head out safely on the water.

» **A café, hotel, beach huts**—this is one resort where you don't have time to get bored.

IMAGE: PMKEXPERT

Secrets

London:

IMAGE: MUSEUM OF LONDON

Map of London 1666

IMAGE: MUSEUM OF LONDON

CREATED BY:
Museum of London
DOWNLOAD LINK:
tinyurl.com/mc-1666london

A fantastic project by the Museum of London, this map reimagines London, England, in 1666—BEFORE the great fire broke out! The map features a number of historical landmarks, some of which no longer exist, including the original London Bridge, the old St. Paul's Cathedral, and the infamous Pudding Lane, where the fire began. An associated audio tour mapped onto Minecraft's in-game records gives you the chance to hear famous voices explain just what you've discovered, while tattered maps can be collected to give you a picture of the city's pre-fire layout. Fantastic fun!

IMAGE: MUSEUM OF LONDON

1666

IMAGE: MUSEUM OF LONDON

DON'T MISS

» The famous **London wall**, fully intact during this period of history.
» The long-lost version of **London Bridge**, with houses stacked on it.
» The original **St. Paul's Cathedral**, which was replaced by the modern version after its destruction.

IMAGE: MUSEUM OF LONDON

IMAGE: MUSEUM OF LONDON

IMAGE: MUSEUM OF LONDON

COOL STUFF

» An **in-game map of the area** means you can find your way around very easily.
» As well as re-creations of buildings from the 1600s, you'll find **cargo ships** on the River Thames.
» **Hundreds of buildings** replicated as they existed before the fire destroyed them.

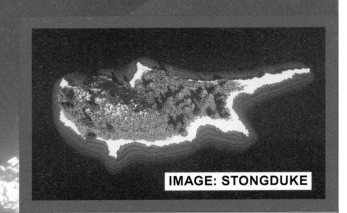

IMAGE: STONGDUKE

CREATED BY:
stongduke
DOWNLOAD LINK:
tinyurl.com/mc-earthmap924

Built as a replica of the ACTUAL surface of the earth, this map exists at a scale of one block for every 924 meters on the ground. Across approximately 16,000 by 32,000 blocks, it re-creates the coastlines and biomes of the world as accurately as possible using real terrain data and painted-on rivers. Find the famous Nile Delta, marvel at added-in landmarks around the globe, and enjoy discovering every country and continent. This map is Survival-friendly, with caves and an End portal, so you can enjoy playing it with your friends!

IMAGE: STONGDUKE

IMAGE: STONGDUKE

1:924 Scale

IMAGE: STONGDUKE

IMAGE: STONGDUKE

IMAGE: STONGDUKE

DON'T MISS

» **Re-creations** of almost every landmass on the globe, from actual data.
» Get a real sense of **scale** for the size of the world by exploring it all.
» **Follow the Nile** from the Mediterranean Sea deep into the heart of Africa.

COOL STUFF

» **Australia**, where the entire outback has been turned into a Badlands biome.
» **The re-creation** of the ancient Stonehenge in England.
» Wherever you live! Can you find your **home country**?

IMAGE: STONGDUKE

Earth Map

Beekeeper's Cottage & Apiary

IMAGE: BLISSCHEN

IMAGE: BLISSCHEN

CREATED BY:
blisschen
DOWNLOAD LINK:
tinyurl.com/mc-beekeepercottage

Most maps that need a resource pack to work don't look very good without one, but blisschen's maps are an exception to that—this quaint beekeeper's cottage retains its cozy charm, looking like something you might stumble on in a fairy tale. Settle down inside and get to work tending your beehives, making and collecting honey while living in harmony with nature. It's a super-relaxing place to explore, and the design of the house is a fantastic one. If you want to get the necessary shaders and resource packs, you can find them all downloadable via the link given above.

IMAGE: BLISSCHEN

IMAGE: BLISSCHEN

IMAGE: BLISSCHEN

DON'T MISS

» **The trees** outside in the garden, teeming with ripe fruit that the bees can't help but enjoy.

» **The boundary walls**, crafted to keep mobs out without making the place feel too fenced in.

» The incredible **interior design**, which only looks better when you add in the resource packs.

IMAGE: BLISSCHEN

COOL STUFF

» If you like this build, you can check out the process of building it on **blisschen's YouTube channel**.

» Further **enhance the map** with resource packs and shaders for the ultimate experience.

» A small but **perfectly formed build** to enjoy and relax in.

IMAGE: BLISSCHEN

CREATED BY:
JorgeTKP
DOWNLOAD LINK:
tinyurl.com/mc-coastaljapan

Built as part of a larger project that was never finished, this coastal Japanese town build is a great example of old and new architecture melded together into a Minecraft world that is both evocative of the past and exciting to explore. Structures in the city include taverns, inns, public bathhouses, hotels, teahouses, and homes, as well as temples and even a sanctuary for the local deity. Everything has both interiors and exteriors, and the city itself is landscaped to perfection—you can spend hours checking out every nook, with always something new to find.

IMAGE: JORGETKP

IMAGE: JORGETKP

IMAGE: JORGETKP

Coastal Japa

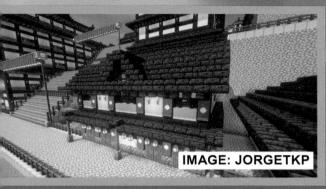

IMAGE: JORGETKP

DON'T MISS

» The **bamboo plantation** secreted alongside one of the houses on the edge of town.

» A **Shinto-style shrine gate** on the outskirts of the map, connecting it to future builds.

» **A huge crane** that implies further construction to come—maybe by you?

IMAGE: JORGETKP

IMAGE: JORGETKP

COOL STUFF

» Tens, if not hundreds, of **old-style Japanese buildings** to explore.

» **Amazing lighting and decoration** make the map look great at night.

» Innovative use of **natural decorations**, both indoors and outdoors.

IMAGE: JORGETKP

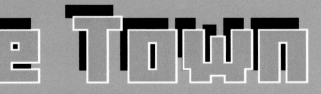

nese Town

Woodland

IMAGE: DREAMWANDERER

IMAGE: DREAMWANDERER

CREATED BY:
DreamWanderer

DOWNLOAD LINK:
tinyurl.com/mc-woodlandlog

Live out your fantasies of being a lone lumberjack in this, the woodland log home. Secreted in a dense forest, this cabin is actually huge, with many different rooms and locations to explore so that you can chill out here indefinitely. With a stone chimney, extra outbuilding, and ultracool interiors, you can hang out here alone or with friends in a map that's perfect for hide-and-seek, horror movie role-play, or just taking ideas from for your own builds. We love the armchairs and kitchen furniture, but there are tons of great interior decoration ideas.

IMAGE: DREAMWANDERER

Log Home

IMAGE: DREAMWANDERER

DON'T MISS

» **The long gravel driveway** through the trees to your log cabin clearing.
» **The hidden storage room** in the attic of the outbuilding.
» **The power generator** outside the main house.

IMAGE: DREAMWANDERER

IMAGE: DREAMWANDERER

IMAGE: DREAMWANDERER

COOL STUFF

» A build made almost entirely **from wood**—keep those flames covered!
» So many pieces of **furniture for you to adapt** and copy in your own builds.
» Incredibly **detailed rooms** and zero laziness when it comes to putting interesting things in the space.

CREATED BY:
BlocksBuild
DOWNLOAD LINK:
tinyurl.com/mc-aztecpyramid

Minecraft's Jungle Pyramids might be exciting to find, but they're not half as impressive as this one, which reimagines the Aztec ruins found in Mexico as if they were still-active, working temples. There's something extremely spooky about heading into the depths of these pyramids—seeing the sacrifices, lava, and offerings—and wondering if you'll ever make it out alive. While exploring, you'll find hidden objects in every level of the pyramid, hinting at the horrors it has endured across time. A fun experience—so long as you're not the one on the altar.

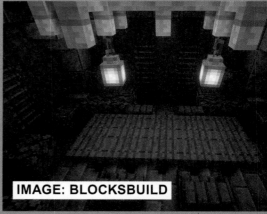

Aztec

IMAGE: BLOCKSBUILD

DON'T MISS

» **The intricate wall decorations** hidden deep within the pyramid.

» **The long stairways** to the top—and the terrifying drop to the bottom.

» **The secret rooms** where the builders would have been sealed in and left to die.

IMAGE: BLOCKSBUILD

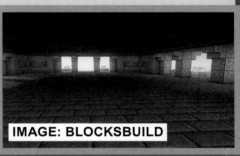

IMAGE: BLOCKSBUILD

IMAGE: BLOCKSBUILD

COOL STUFF

» **A "living" exterior**, filled with grass and flowers, giving the impression of an extremely old place.

» **Still-burning torches**, suggesting that this temple might not be as abandoned as it first seems.

» **Hidden rooms** all over the place, just like you'd expect to find in a real temple.

Pyramid

English Cou

IMAGE: BLISSCHEN

CREATED BY:
blisschen
DOWNLOAD LINK:
tinyurl.com/mc-englishcountryhouse

Another build from blisschen that looks its best with a number of mods and resource packs installed, the English Country House is nonetheless a fantastic creation. With a backstory of a centuries-old curse, it can be explored to your heart's content, or you can enjoy the design and build process on blisschen's YouTube channel. This map is a particularly intense one for such a small build, so take care if your PC isn't very powerful—especially if you're installing all the necessary mods and packs. Either way, there's a lot to like in this well-crafted mansion house build—get exploring!

IMAGE: BLISSCHEN

IMAGE: BLISSCHEN

ntry House

IMAGE: BLISSCHEN

DON'T MISS
» A fantastic **fireplace** with picture frames hanging above it and a rug in front.
» A **well-stocked kitchen** with every appliance and surface you could need.
» **Unfurnished bedrooms**, just waiting for you to move into them.

IMAGE: BLISSCHEN

IMAGE: BLISSCHEN

IMAGE: BLISSCHEN

COOL STUFF
» Looks especially great with the **extra mods** and packs installed.
» Perfectly crafted **wildflower gardens** in the grounds frame the house beautifully.
» Fantastic **location** in a world where you can play any mode you desire.

Sorcery & Sci-Fi Builds

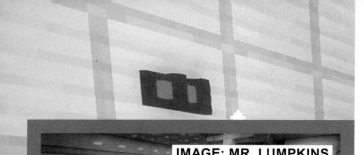
IMAGE: MR. LUMPKINS

CREATED BY:
Mr. Lumpkins
DOWNLOAD LINK:
tinyurl.com/mc-robotfactory

Transport yourself into the distant future of Minecraft with this Robot Factory build! Small but perfectly formed, this map places you in the center of an industrialized future where robot construction is the only job available to you! Explore the assembly floor with its population of workers and robots of different types and sizes, or observe the whole thing from the administration and security offices. There are plenty of impressive flourishes in this map despite its small size, and that's why we think you should check it out as soon as possible!

IMAGE: MR. LUMPKINS

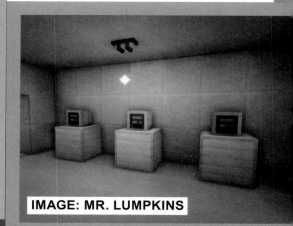
IMAGE: MR. LUMPKINS

The Robot

IMAGE: MR. LUMPKINS

DON'T MISS

» **The WORKING robotic arms**, made possible through smart use of command blocks.
» The many different **interactive elements** on the **assembly floor**.
» The **security camera** in the **admin suite** that actually allows you to spy on other workers.

IMAGE: MR. LUMPKINS

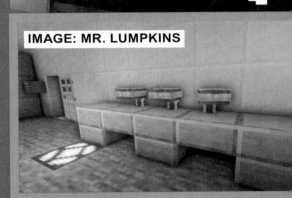

IMAGE: MR. LUMPKINS

COOL STUFF

» Huge amounts of creativity shown in the use of **command blocks**.
» **Customized textures** and resources designed to make the map even more futuristic.
» **Transparent design**, so you can figure out how the most complicated stuff is done!

IMAGE: MR. LUMPKINS

Factory

Future City

CREATED BY:
Zeemo

DOWNLOAD LINK: tinyurl.com/mc-futurecity

We guarantee you've never seen a build like this in Minecraft before. Step into the future of the Overworld with this futuristic city creation from Zeemo. An absolutely humongous build spanning thousands of blocks, you could explore it for days without seeing everything. A download area, a military base, futuristic skyscrapers, and a geodesic biome are just some of the incredible sights you'll find here. We can only imagine the world that would create such marvels! If you need advice, just pick a direction and fly—you're guaranteed to see something amazing.

IMAGE: ZEEMO

IMAGE: ZEEMO

IMAGE: ZEEMO

DON'T MISS

» **The biodome area**, with a dome so huge it contains multiple skyscrapers.
» **Futuristic vehicles** docked all around the city, from boats to aircraft.
» **A tunnel network** that crisscrosses the city and allows for speedy access all around it.

IMAGE: ZEEMO

IMAGE: ZEEMO

COOL STUFF

» **A huge city** with a complete infrastructure, unlike anything you've ever seen before.
» **Amazing architecture** and huge buildings to explore and colonize alone or with friends.
» Literally hours of fun to be had exploring the **farthest reaches of this world**.

IMAGE: ZEEMO

IMAGE: ZEEMO

steampunk

IMAGE: CLOSEEDBR

CREATED BY:
CloseeDBr

DOWNLOAD LINK:
tinyurl.com/mc-steampunkmansion

The past meets (a different version of) the future in a Victorian world where amazing contraptions take over! This mansion is far from the typical idea of one: with a small footprint, it towers up high, branching out into larger and more sophisticated floors while being supported by a network of poles and supports. It's a twisty, turny labyrinth of features that you can have fun looking around, imagining the sort of person who might (or does!) live here. Futuristic meets fantasy in the best possible way.

IMAGE: CLOSEEDBR

IMAGE: CLOSEEDBR

Mansion

IMAGE: CLOSEEDBR

DON'T MISS

» The various **suits of armor** dotted around—ideal gear if you're playing in Survival mode.

» **The map** showing the **mansion and its surrounding area** so you can take excursions.

» **Stacks of resources** just piled up—**diamonds, gold, netherite**—all you could ever need!

IMAGE: CLOSEEDBR

IMAGE: CLOSEEDBR

IMAGE: CLOSEEDBR

COOL STUFF

» A steam-powered imagination of the future—that's what the **windmill's** for.

» The **balconies** on every level, which somehow give you a view of the house FROM the house.

» Around **eight levels**, including a creepy basement area and a roof-level viewing deck.

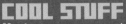

IMAGE: DANI4355

CREATED BY:
Dani4355
DOWNLOAD LINK:
tinyurl.com/mc-villagecastle

A castle is always fun to build in Minecraft—but in real life, they were usually there to protect something. This map replicates that exact feel by placing a castle on a mountain overlooking a village in need of protection. There are 20 buildings, including the castle, a church, blacksmith's, windmill, bakery, watchtower, coal mine, and more besides! Populated with villagers, this is a cool place to do your medieval role-play or for building yet more defenses. It's a perfect size for just a few people to play in, so check it out—we think you'll have a great time.

IMAGE: DANI4355

IMAGE: DANI4355

Medieval Village

IMAGE: DANI4355

DON'T MISS

» The stunning **windmill design** found next to one of the farm areas.
» A well inside the **castle forecourt**—but what's at the bottom of it?
» **Plenty of gold blocks**, stored in the **church** for (ahem) easy access.

IMAGE: DANI4355

IMAGE: DANI4355

COOL STUFF

» A realistically sized **working village**, not too big, not too small.
» Built in a captivating **landscape with plenty of biomes** in close reach.
» **A castle** that looks and feels like something that could actually have existed in real life.

IMAGE: DANI4355

with Castle

Vales of

CREATED BY: qwryzu
DOWNLOAD LINK:
tinyurl.com/mc-valesofamoril

A Tolkien-esque landscape awaits you in the Vales of Amoril map, which is untouched by human construction but instead exists as a blank canvas onto which you can put your stamp, whether that's building a city or a small monument to mark the places you stopped on your way through. At 10,000 by 10,000 blocks, this build is so gigantic we could only show off tiny portions of its truly majestic scope. Voyage across rolling hills, steep mountains, huge flowing rivers, and tiny brooks, through grasslands and forests, fjords, glaciers, and bays—it's truly impressive how realistic Minecraft can look.

IMAGE: QWRYZU

IMAGE: QWRYZU

IMAGE: QWRYZU

Amoril

IMAGE: QWRYZU

DON'T MISS

» **The water system** of rivers and streams connecting together and heading for the ocean.
» **Mountain ranges** providing incredible vistas to marvel at.
» **Well-protected islands** that make the ideal place to set up a safe base.

IMAGE: QWRYZU

IMAGE: QWRYZU

COOL STUFF

» **Landscape** scaled up to resemble the size of an actual landscape.
» **Ultrarealistic biome features**, from river deltas to ice floes.
» The perfect setting for a **long-form role-play** or **quest adventure**.

IMAGE: QWRYZU

IMAGE: JUSTIN TIRRELL

CREATED BY:
Justin Tirrell

DOWNLOAD LINK:
tinyurl.com/mc-towerofallabove

Built as the central hub for a great fantasy nation, the Tower of All Above is a monument to knowledge and power, stretching high above the clouds and capable of housing hundreds. From the grand hall at the bottom to the library above, and the armory and conference chamber at the top, this is a build with a huge amount to explore and something to impress at every stage. Whether you want to use it in your own build or just explore someone else's creation, it's a must-see for fantasy lovers.

IMAGE: JUSTIN TIRRELL

IMAGE: JUSTIN TIRRELL

The Tower

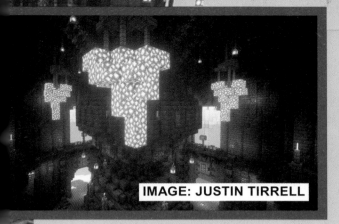

IMAGE: JUSTIN TIRRELL

DON'T MISS

» **The golems** protecting the most important levels, ensuring peace throughout the tower.

» **The shining beacons** at the top of the tower, firing colored light into the sky.

» **Enchanting tables**, furnaces, and other crafting stations dotted all around for you to use.

IMAGE: JUSTIN TIRRELL

IMAGE: JUSTIN TIRRELL

COOL STUFF

» **Plenty of rooms** to explore, each with its own function and inhabitants.

» **Stunning architecture** and design, from the armor halls to the grand pedestals.

» A **great backstory** that can be seen in every element of the build.

IMAGE: JUSTIN TIRRELL

# of All Above

USS Ente

DOWNLOAD LINK:
tinyurl.com/mc-starship

This Star Trek themed build re-creates the iconic starship *Enterprise* at a life-size scale. That means for every meter on the "real" ship, there's one block in the build, making this so huge we could barely even fit it into our screenshots! The exterior is wonderfully detailed and the size is truly epic. And when you break inside the shell, you realize that you can see how it was built if you want to re-create it, or fill the empty space with your own decks, engines, and more. Either way, it's up to you—you're the captain now!

IMAGE: ASTRALSAPPHIRE

IMAGE: ASTRALSAPPHIRE

IMAGE: ASTRALSAPPHIRE

DON'T MISS

» **The bridge area**, located at the very top of the saucer section.
» **Phaser banks** distributed at strategic points throughout the build.
» **The glowing engines** in the nacelles, ready for warp speed!

IMAGE: ASTRALSAPPHIRE

IMAGE: ASTRALSAPPHIRE

IMAGE: ASTRALSAPPHIRE

COOL STUFF

» An unbelievably huge re-creation of a beloved **starship** almost everyone will recognize.
» Plenty of **space** to expand and modify the build so you can put your own stamp on it.
» **Build-assisting features** left in, so you can see what it truly takes to make a build this size.

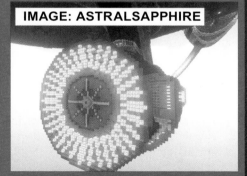
IMAGE: ASTRALSAPPHIRE

Mars Colony

CREATED BY: Antigod
DOWNLOAD LINK: tinyurl.com/mc-marscolony

Now Minecraft can take you where no one has gone before—to Mars, the red planet! This build is a reasonably realistic version of what a Mars landing base might look like, with a few small modular habitats, a rover for getting around, and a satellite for sending and receiving communications. We might not have made a manned mission to our closest planetary neighbor just yet, but when we do, the base will probably look a lot like this one! Explore, build on, or just hike your way around this custom Martian landscape for the ultimate space adventure. The maker says they'd been watching a lot of space films, which gave them the inspiration to build this Mars-themed colony. It has living places, a huge biodome full of plants, and a central workshop where the astronauts farm, build, and plan everything.

IMAGE: ANTIGOD

IMAGE: ANTIGOD

IMAGE: ANTIGOD

DON'T MISS

» The **biodome habitat pod**, where food is growing in an artificial Earth landscape.

» **The Mars rover**, which could transport astronauts to and from all areas of the surface.

» **The craters and mountains** of an unspoiled Martian surface, now yours to explore.

IMAGE: ANTIGOD

IMAGE: ANTIGOD

IMAGE: ANTIGOD

IMAGE: ANTIGOD

COOL STUFF

» Completely **customized landscape**, designed to resemble the actual landscape of Mars.

» Several **purpose-built buildings** to explore, with real thinking behind the base's layout.

» A small but **perfectly formed map** that should work great on PCs of any kind.

IMAGE: TRYDAR

CREATED BY:
Trydar
DOWNLOAD LINK:
tinyurl.com/mc-spacetelescope

Space telescopes are about as futuristic as modern engineering gets, on the very edge of what's possible with the technological and scientific knowledge we've collected as a civilization over thousands of years—so why shouldn't Minecraft have its own? This tutorial map comes in tandem with a YouTube video (accessible via the link above) that shows you how to make this map on your own, if you want to! There isn't much to do other than marvel at quite how cool this design is, but if you want to make a base on a satellite, then it makes a great start for that, at least!

IMAGE: TRYDAR

IMAGE: TRYDAR

Futuristic Spa

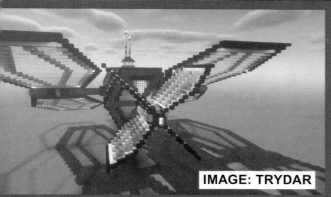

IMAGE: TRYDAR

DON'T MISS

» The **little menu** showing exactly what blocks the telescope is made of, and how many there are.

» The **giant glowing sensor** found inside the telescope's main optical barrel.

» The **angled solar panels** that power the build and that you can hike all the way up.

IMAGE: TRYDAR

IMAGE: TRYDAR

COOL STUFF

» A complete guide to building your own **space telescope** creation—copy or modify it!

» **Multiple versions** of the telescope, so you can see exactly how it was made.

» A truly **impressive scale** of build and a spur to imagine bigger!

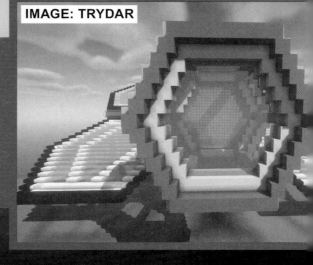

IMAGE: TRYDAR

ce Telescope

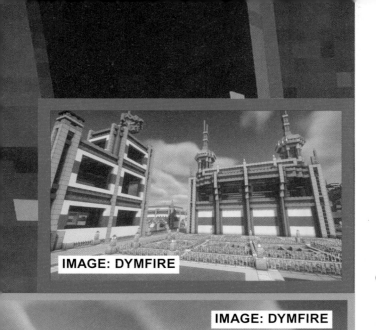

IMAGE: DYMFIRE

CREATED BY:
DymFire
DOWNLOAD LINK:
tinyurl.com/mc-marssite325

Another build imagining life on Mars, this one goes much further into the future! In this world, we don't just have a base on the red planet—there's an entire city there! Filled with purpose-built rooms like barracks, tech labs, vehicle storage, and water treatment plants, there's so much to explore and discover—although, weirdly, no people. Is there a mystery to solve? The creator isn't telling, but that's enough of a reason to go check it out, as far as we're concerned . . .

IMAGE: DYMFIRE

IMAGE: DYMFIRE

Mars Site

IMAGE: DYMFIRE

DON'T MISS

» **The dropships and landing vehicles** that make it seem like you just reached the planet.

» **The Mars rover** docked in one of the vehicle garages, just waiting to be taken out.

» So many buildings to explore, all fully kitted out. Can you find the **terrarium**?

IMAGE: DYMFIRE

IMAGE: DYMFIRE

COOL STUFF

» A huge **base to explore**, set in an alien landscape of canyons and mountains.

» **Custom-built blocks** and models to give extra flavor to the world.

» **Huge structures** built on a truly impressive scale.

IMAGE: DYMFIRE

#325

Survival & Adventure Maps

In this map, you're stuck on a raft in the middle of the ocean with only a few blocks and a chest for company. Around you, debris appears that can help you in your efforts—but can you survive before the mobs start coming or you perish from starvation?! This is a ruthlessly simple build that uses its limited resources to great effect. From the seafloor to the sky, you'll need to use everything you can get your hands on in order to survive in this extremely tough environment.

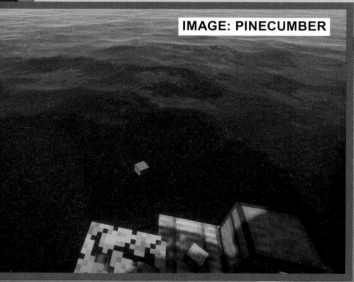

Raft Su

DON'T MISS

» The **shipwrecks** nearby—maybe your only source of actual loot.

» The **iron ore** that floats by—you're going to need it!

» A **fishing rod** in the chest, which gives you your best chance to eat.

IMAGE: PINECUMBER

IMAGE: PINECUMBER

IMAGE: PINECUMBER

COOL STUFF

» When you're in the water, you have **stamina**—so don't run out!

» Entirely **command-block-based** behavior means it's mod-free!

» **Debris floats** past as if the raft is moving for an awesome real-life effect.

IMAGE: PINECUMBER

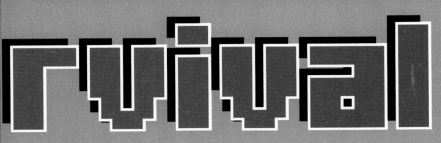

MAZES

IMAGE: NEREID REGULUS

CREATED BY:
Nereid Regulus
DOWNLOAD LINK:
tinyurl.com/mc-mazeescapist

An incredible "complete the monument" map that places you in a giant labyrinth with a simple goal: collect all 16 wools while the maze layout shifts around you. Filled with NPCs, powerful gear, and dangerous enemies, this open-world experience is great as a solo or multiplayer map, and is deliberately very difficult, with as many as 30 hours of gameplay promised! If you're a fan of puzzles or exploration, this is the perfect map for you—just make sure you follow the rules, and enjoy!

Page 1 of 2

These weird doors in the cave near the forest are really intriguing... Everyday another one opens and the one before closes. It looks like the number on the door matches with the number of days I've been here, and once all eight doors have passed, the cycle repeats. So on day 9,

Done

IMAGE: NEREID REGULUS

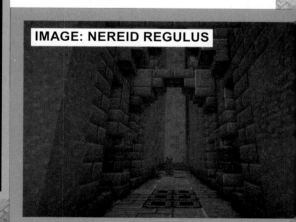

IMAGE: NEREID REGULUS

capist

IMAGE: NEREID REGULUS

IMAGE: NEREID REGULUS

DON'T MISS

» **Chests** dotted around in some dead ends—you'll need the gear inside!
» **The lore,** contained in the books found around the map.
» An insane **swamp area** where witches ride around on top of phantoms.

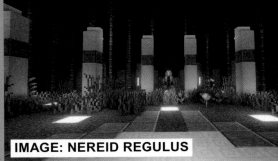

IMAGE: NEREID REGULUS

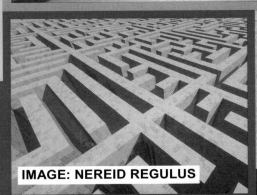

IMAGE: NEREID REGULUS

COOL STUFF

» A truly **colossal maze** that weaves in and out of the landscape, even underground.
» Varies between **megastructures** and **tiny maze corridors**.
» **Brilliant architecture** in the areas you have to explore.

97

ODD 100 ONE

Trivia maps are a really fun addition to the pantheon of Minecraft games, and this might well be the grandfather of them all. Face off against no fewer than 100 different odd-one-out games, strung together in succession. Your goal is to make the smallest number of wrong answers ever, to achieve the rank of pro Minecrafter. Along the way, you'll find sample rooms and clues/hints dotted around to help you if you get stuck. A super-fun single-player experience—and one you can try over and over.

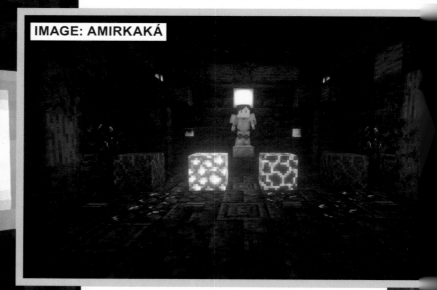
IMAGE: AMIRKAKÁ

IMAGE: AMIRKAKÁ

IMAGE: AMIRKAKÁ

IMAGE: AMIRKAKÁ

DON'T MISS

» The **creepy armor stand mannequins** that tell you whether you're right or wrong.
» **Buttons to push** in order to signal the odd one out—no further instructions needed!
» The **secrets and hidden details** that you have to remember for future quizzes!

IMAGE: AMIRKAKÁ

COOL STUFF

» **Fantastically designed rooms** with clear and simple challenges to beat.
» Each level containing a **small biome** of its own, with potential hints hidden inside.
» An **exciting challenge** aimed at new and old players alike.

IMAGE: AMIRKAKÁ

IMAGE: HANSRINALDI

CREATED BY: HansRinaldi
DOWNLOAD LINK:
tinyurl.com/mc-adventure1

A bespoke Survival island landscape, Adventure Island is perfectly crafted to provide a fun and challenging experience in Survival mode, in a setting that Minecraft would never generate on its own. The map contains two large islands separated by a river, with smaller islands scattered around it. There are only a few hidden structures around to add flavor, but nothing that will upset an attempt to play the Survival game. A fantastic place to get a fresh experience in a familiar game mode!

IMAGE: HANSRINALDI

IMAGE: HANSRINALDI

Adventu

IMAGE: HANSRINALDI

DON'T MISS

» Realistic **volcanic island landscapes** for playing a Survival game on.

» **Bespoke-crafted terrains** that look beautiful against the sea.

» **The beach** surrounding the islands naturally fades into a grassy landscape.

IMAGE: HANSRINALDI

IMAGE: HANSRINALDI

IMAGE: HANSRINALDI

COOL STUFF

» The **smallish lagoon island**, perfect for setting up a well-fortified base on.

» A huge number of **jungle trees** providing shelter, food, and resources.

» **The lava lake**—a source of both potential smelting fuel and obsidian for a portal.

IMAGE: HANSRINALDI

re Island

Parkour

CREATED BY:
TBC_Miles
DOWNLOAD LINK:
tinyurl.com/mc-parkourspiral

You haven't truly played Minecraft until you've tackled a parkour map, and this one is as punishing as they get! Built in the shape of a giant tower, the parkour area spirals around the central column, broken into levels themed after different biomes, structures, and terrains. Slip up and you'll lose a little progress, but it's pretty forgiving—and it has to be, given how hard things will get as you ascend! Challenging, original, and varied—a great parkour map, no matter how good you think you are!

IMAGE: TBC_MILES

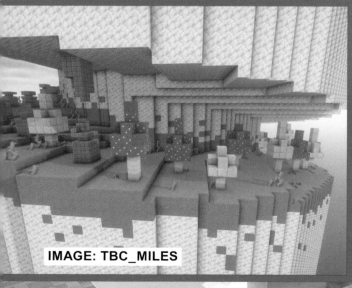

IMAGE: TBC_MILES

IMAGE: TBC_MILES

Spiral

IMAGE: TBC_MILES

DON'T MISS

» **The Nether section**, which takes you through each major biome of the Nether.

» **Floating jump puzzles**—it's a long way down!

» **The pink mushroom zone**, which uses familiar blocks to create stunning new visuals.

IMAGE: TBC_MILES

IMAGE: TBC_MILES

IMAGE: TBC_MILES

COOL STUFF

» A truly **huge number of levels** to play in, each with its own theme.

» Environments that replicate **Minecraft biomes**, and many that are wholly original!

» The **tower changes color** to help you realize how far through it you are.

IMAGE: NOTMIKEWEIR

CREATED BY:
Notmikeweir
DOWNLOAD LINK:
tinyurl.com/mc-archipelago

The Archipelago is a mystery-based map that blends survival, puzzle, and combat elements in a mysterious landscape themed around multiple island builds. Collect gold, diamonds, and other loot from the different areas of the map. Complete parkour and explore dungeons as you race to find the mysterious tropical loot. With a few story elements that unfold as you explore, this is a great experience for single players or small parties. And, let's face it, the build is impressive even before you factor in all of that!

IMAGE: NOTMIKEWEIR

IMAGE: NOTMIKEWEIR

The Archi

IMAGE: NOTMIKEWEIR

DON'T MISS

» The **large ship** in the harbor of one of the seaport islands.
» A **fortress with impressive walls** protecting a small fishing village.
» The incredible areas to explore, with secret goals such as the **heart of the mountain**!

IMAGE: NOTMIKEWEIR

IMAGE: NOTMIKEWEIR

COOL STUFF

» A story that unfolds as you **explore different parts** of the map, highlighting your true goal.
» Dozens of **interesting areas to explore**, each one suitable for spotlighting on its own!
» **Custom-built structures** and **natural features**, all of which add to the otherworldly feeling.

IMAGE: NOTMIKEWEIR

pelago

CREATED BY:
HansRinaldi
DOWNLOAD LINK:
tinyurl.com/mc-junglecliffs

This pure Survival map reimagines Minecraft's world as an expansive jungle island, unlike anything that would appear in the game naturally. With a secret base to find and a deep lagoon set in the mountaintop, there's plenty to do in this world, whether you're building, exploring, or simply hoping to marvel at the scenery. Watch out for pandas as you explore, because there are plenty of them around, and try not to disrupt the ecosystem too badly with whatever you do here!

IMAGE: HANSRINALDI

IMAGE: HANSRINALDI

IMAGE: HANSRINALDI

Jungle

IMAGE: HANSRINALDI

DON'T MISS

» **Incredible cliffs and amazing meadows** sharing the jungle island landscape.

» The **stunning scenery** of the lagoon that sits in the top of the mountain caldera.

» The **secret base** hidden somewhere around the island—can you figure out how to find it?

IMAGE: HANSRINALDI

IMAGE: HANSRINALDI

COOL STUFF

» **Custom scenery** on a huge Survival island that you can explore and utilize at your own pace.

» Tons of **native mobs**, including lots of the usually elusive panda varieties!

» A simple but effective use of a **single-biome world** with fantastic visuals.

IMAGE: HANSRINALDI

CLIFFS

CREATED BY:
Serpentem_Malfoy

DOWNLOAD LINK: tinyurl.com/mc-rpgadventure

Where most maps build a small area, the RPG adventure map goes full Middle Earth on Minecraft, with a 25,000-block transformation into a totally new fantasy world filled with newly imagined biomes. Explore the honey caves and ice caverns, look around the inside of an extinct volcano, and visit dwarven ruins and custom-built forests and villages in the shadow of giant mushrooms the likes of which you've never seen. We couldn't possibly tell you everything there is to explore here—suffice it to say it'll take you months to see it all!

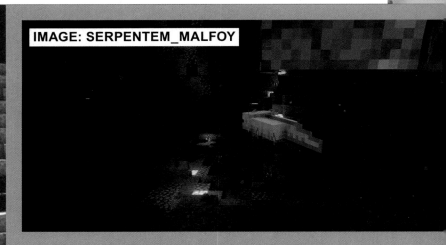
IMAGE: SERPENTEM_MALFOY

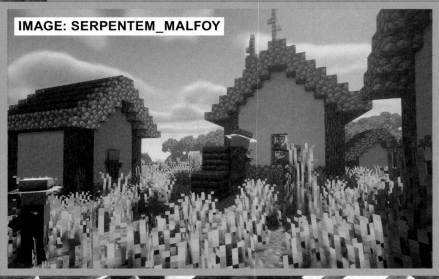
IMAGE: SERPENTEM_MALFOY

IMAGE: SERPENTEM_MALFOY

DON'T MISS

» **New landscapes** like the autumnal forests, frozen mountain peaks, and winding sea caves.

» The stunning **flower forest**, reimagined with giant blooms replacing normal trees.

» The inclusion of the latest biomes, such as **lush caves** hidden beneath the world.

COOL STUFF

» Totally **reimagined landscape**, built from scratch and reusing almost nothing but villages.

» A map with a **truly epic scale**, guaranteed to be larger than almost anything else you've seen.

» More **biomes** than you could ever hope to see in the normal game.

IMAGE: SERPENTEM_MALFOY

IMAGE: SERPENTEM_MALFOY

IMAGE: SERPENTEM_MALFOY

Parkour City

DOWNLOAD LINK: tinyurl.com/mc-parkourcity

Parkour fans who are getting bored of natural landscapes or abstract challenges, this is the map for you! Parkour City is a midsize map where you run, jump, and plummet your way around a parkour course wherein all the elements are integrated into a city. Travel over vehicles, ledges, walls, and construction machinery to reach your goals! With an auto-respawn and checkpoint system, it's easy to play for beginners but challenging enough for experienced players, and its impressive urban landscape means it truly meets the criteria of an epic build.

IMAGE: ZOMBIE1111

IMAGE: ZOMBIE1111

IMAGE: ZOMBIE1111

IMAGE: ZOMBIE1111

COOL STUFF

» This map is **multiplayer-friendly**, so you can test your skill alone or race your friends through a speedrun!

» More than **50 different secrets** to find if you'd rather take it slow and explore.

» A **ghost mode** for people who just want to explore or watch others play the map.

DON'T MISS

» The **unlockable areas** that you can only reach by finding secrets.

» The fact that you can **customize the difficulty level** if you struggle!

» . . . any of the platforms **when you jump!**

IMAGE: ZOMBIE1111

IMAGE: ZOMBIE1111

Escape It

IMAGE: ELITEPHU

IMAGE: ELITEPHU

CREATED BY:
ElitePhu
DOWNLOAD LINK:
tinyurl.com/mc-escapetheroom

Room escape games are super popular right now, and there are tons in the Minecraft community alone—but it takes something more than that to reach the criteria of epic, and this map definitely does that! This isn't just one escape room, but no fewer than eight separate ones, each of which requires all your cunning, skill, and smarts to allow you to progress to the next area. Better yet, the creator is aiming for 25 levels in total, so who knows how many there'll be by the time you download this?!

IMAGE: ELITEPHU

The Room

IMAGE: ELITEPHU

DON'T MISS

» A **hard-to-find secret** hidden in every level—just locate, then click on the sign!

» The **ACTUAL snowman** in the winter-themed area—move over, snow golem!

» The **mining town** area, containing avatars of the level's creators!

IMAGE: ELITEPHU

IMAGE: ELITEPHU

COOL STUFF

» **Themed escape rooms** and a hub-world/lobby to explore with bonus parkour levels.

» A massive **variety of puzzles** and landscapes to get your teeth into.

» **Innovative and original puzzles**, for single players or groups to solve.

IMAGE: ELITEPHU

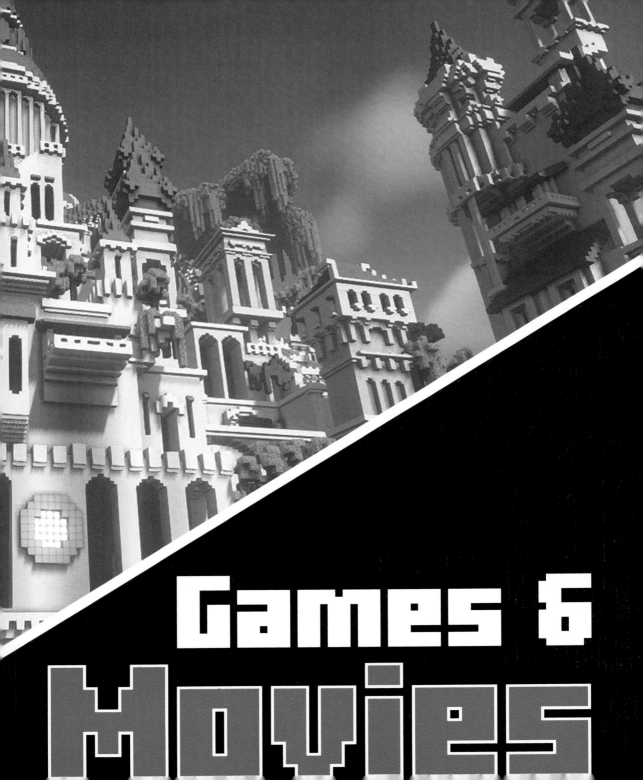

Games & Movies

CREATED BY:
dennisbuilds
DOWNLOAD LINK:
tinyurl.com/mc-monumentvalley

Inspired by the stunning mobile game *Monument Valley*, this map features a selection of tall buildings linked by walkways and arches with Greek style architecture that extends toward the sky. Reimagined as an ancient port city, the dizzying locations from the game are all recognizable here. Whether you've played the game or not, you can appreciate the sheer aesthetic beauty of this creation and its buildings, making it a fantastic map to bask in. Put on your pointed hat and go explore the Monument Valley—just watch out for crows!

IMAGE: DENNISBUILDS

IMAGE: DENNISBUILDS

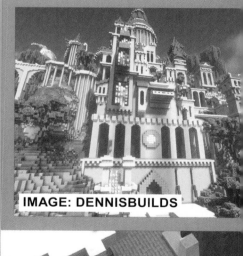

IMAGE: DENNISBUILDS

Monument

IMAGE: DENNISBUILDS

DON'T MISS

» The **massive sailing ship** in the port, where you can find secrets and items to gather.

» A huge **angel statue**, sculpted out of marble and stone and reaching toward the sky.

» The **giant glass globe** that surrounds a glowing orb—but then, it's impossible to ignore!

IMAGE: DENNISBUILDS

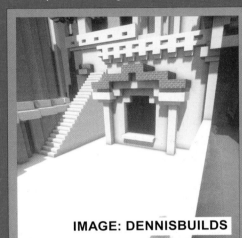

IMAGE: DENNISBUILDS

COOL STUFF

» An **impressive re-creation** of a game that has building design and architecture at its heart.

» **Stunning locations** that'll give you hours of exploration fun.

» **Attention to detail** in the structures, with care placed in everything from the smallest doorway to the tallest tower.

IMAGE: DENNISBUILDS

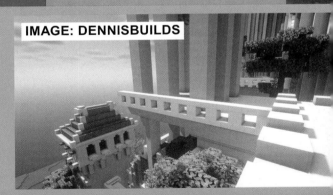

Valley

Sonic the

CREATED BY:
Disco_
DOWNLOAD LINK:
tinyurl.com/mc-sonicthehedgehog

As surely one of the world's most recognizable video game characters, Sonic the Hedgehog's home—the iconic Green Hill Zone—is almost as well-known as he is. Now, for probably the first time, you can explore a 3D realization of the familiar location in all its 8-bit glory. From the classic palm trees to the unmistakable power-up TVs, this map has everything a *Sonic the Hedgehog* fan could ever ask for and then some. It's got everything except the music, and we dare you not to hum it to yourself as you jump around!

IMAGE: DISCO_

IMAGE: DISCO_

IMAGE: DISCO

Hedgehog

IMAGE: DISCO_

DON'T MISS

» **Parkour sections** that resemble the actual gameplay of *Sonic the Hedgehog*.

» **Secret messages** hidden around the map to clue you in to trivia about this world.

» The **beautifully re-created flora** that retains its 8-bit charm even in 3D.

IMAGE: DISCO_

IMAGE: DISCO_

IMAGE: DISCO_

COOL STUFF

» Surely as complete a re-creation of a *Sonic* level as you can make in Minecraft.

» Painstakingly rendered and game-accurate versions of **platforms, grass, bumpers, and more**.

» **No corners cut** in making this look as much like *Sonic* as it can.

IMAGE: SALESTRO

CREATED BY:
Salestro
DOWNLOAD LINK:
tinyurl.com/mc-theskeld

If you love Minecraft, you probably like *Among Us,* too—after all, it has taken the gaming world by storm in a way that almost no other game besides Minecraft ever has! This map re-creates the iconic *Among Us* map The Skeld, giving you the chance to roam freely around a fully 3D version of the spaceship itself, complete with engine room, cockpit, cafeteria area, and more! Whether you want to role-play *Among Us* or just get a sense for what these locations would be like in a more realistic world, this map gives you everything you need!

IMAGE: SALESTRO

IMAGE: SALESTRO

Among Us:

IMAGE: SALESTRO

DON'T MISS

» The **cockpit area**, where multiple players can look out onto an empty sky.
» Even the familiar **emergency meeting button** has been included!
» **Small Easter eggs** that you'll remember from the actual *Among Us* rooms.

IMAGE: SALESTRO

IMAGE: SALESTRO

COOL STUFF

» Near-perfect re-creation of the familiar location from ***Among Us***.
» The ability to **view the map** from above to get a good sense of where everything is.
» **Masses of detail** in every room—you can't do tasks, but you'll feel like you can!

IMAGE: SALESTRO

The Skeld

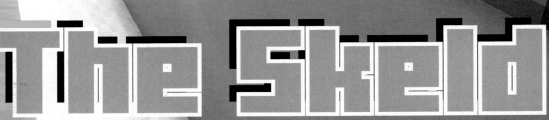

Zelda: Link's

IMAGE: PICKLEDSCONES

IMAGE: PICKLEDSCONES

CREATED BY:
pickledscones

DOWNLOAD LINK:
tinyurl.com/mc-zelda1

The Legend of Zelda is a beloved franchise, and this map takes the unforgettable Koholint Island from *Link's Awakening* (the 1993 Game Boy version) and renders it into a fully 3D environment, replete with scratch-built redstone and command-block-powered behavior, and customized textures and graphical resources. Explorable and playable, this map even allows you to play the first five dungeons, with mobs and assets made just for the conversion. A stunning effort from some committed fans.

IMAGE: PICKLEDSCONES

Awakening

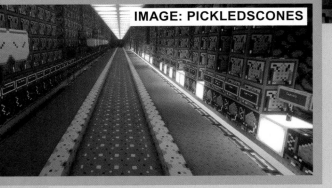

IMAGE: PICKLEDSCONES

DON'T MISS

» Secrets and Easter eggs every *Zelda* **player** will appreciate.

» The cut-scenes, re-creating those found in the original edition of *Link's Awakening*.

» The **giant egg** on a mountaintop, rendered in full 3D for the first time!

IMAGE: PICKLEDSCONES

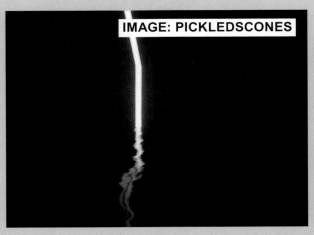

IMAGE: PICKLEDSCONES

COOL STUFF

» **Fun menu system**—enter the cartridges into the in-world Game Boy to continue!

» Beautifully redrawn **custom textures** for almost every block in the map.

» An intricately created system of **command blocks** means it works without extra downloads.

IMAGE: PICKLEDSCONES

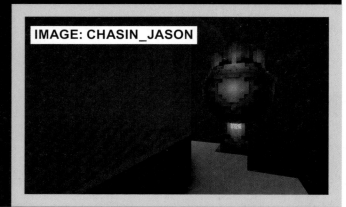

IMAGE: CHASIN_JASON

CREATED BY:
Chasin_Jason
DOWNLOAD LINK:
tinyurl.com/mc-superminecraft

Super Mario Galaxy is one of the best Mario games ever made, and with its unusual planet-based worlds, it was just ripe for a Minecraft re-creation. This map—Super Minecraft Galaxy—brings it to life in true Minecraft style! Even more impressive, it doesn't just remake the map: it's also got the game in there, too, with 86 stars to collect and every basic mission in the game re-created. We're feeling exhausted just thinking about all that work, but luckily you can just load it up and enjoy!

IMAGE: CHASIN_JASON

IMAGE: CHASIN_JASON

Super Minec

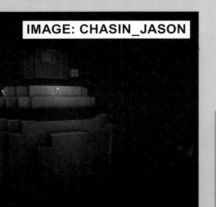

IMAGE: CHASIN_JASON

DON'T MISS

» The buttons that **launch the stars** and kick off the gameplay triggers.
» Item frames containing **power-ups** and items for you to snag.
» The classic Mario gameplay, such as **item blocks** and stars to collect!

IMAGE: CHASIN_JASON

COOL STUFF

» Re-creates both the locations AND the gameplay of the beloved *Super Mario Galaxy*.
» Expertly designed to resemble *Super Mario Galaxy* as much as possible—no small feat!
» Simple to start playing, but **hours of fun** once you get going.

IMAGE: CHASIN_JASON

raft Galaxy

Genshin Impact

IMAGE: BLISSCHEN

IMAGE: BLISSCHEN

CREATED BY:
blisschen
DOWNLOAD LINK:
tinyurl.com/mc-genshin

New to the gaming scene, *Genshin Impact* has nonetheless made a huge splash—and now you can make a splash, thanks to blisschen's re-creation of the unforgettable Dawn Winery, as seen in the game. As with all blisschen's maps, this looks better with mods, but it's still beautiful regardless, giving you the ability to visit this calm winery and see all that it has to offer. A great map to explore whether you're a *Genshin Impact* player or not!

IMAGE: BLISSCHEN

Dawn Winery

IMAGE: BLISSCHEN

DON'T MISS
» The **secret nooks and crannies** in the grounds of the winery.
» Some **fantastic furniture** and interior decoration.
» The **empty room upstairs** just waiting for you to set up a base!

IMAGE: BLISSCHEN

IMAGE: BLISSCHEN

COOL STUFF
» **Stunningly crafted scenery** and structures, instantly recognizable from the game.
» **Beautifully landscaped grounds** around the winery building itself.
» An even better experience if you install the **mods listed** on the page linked above.

IMAGE: BLISSCHEN

Hobbit Hole

CREATED BY: JayLithical
DOWNLOAD LINK: tinyurl.com/mc-hobbithole

Whether you enjoy The Lord of the Rings world direct from Tolkien's books, the movies, or that rather odd cartoon from the '70s, you'll recognize the idea of a Hobbit Hole—the preferred dwellings of Hobbits in Middle Earth. This incredibly cozy and well-decorated home can serve as an excellent starter base or be used as inspiration for builds you make around the same theme. Beautifully rendered using stock assets, it just goes to show what you can accomplish in Minecraft in a day, without extra bells and whistles provided by mods and resource packs.

IMAGE: JAYLITHICAL

IMAGE: JAYLITHICAL

IMAGE: JAYLITHICAL

DON'T MISS

» The **beautiful furniture** and interior decoration.

» An **enchanting table, weapons, armor, and supplies**—start your Survival game here!

» The customized **End portal** hidden in one of the rooms.

IMAGE: JAYLITHICAL

IMAGE: JAYLITHICAL

COOL STUFF

» A build that's both quaint and impressive, brought to life by its **position in the landscape**.

» Fantastic **attention to detail**, with not a single piece of scenery out of place.

» Imaginative use of **familiar assets** to create a unique feel and aesthetic.

IMAGE: JAYLITHICAL

IMAGE: JAYLITHICAL

129

CREATED BY:
ShadowPlayz95
DOWNLOAD LINK:
tinyurl.com/mc-tatooine

IMAGE: SHADOWPLAYZ95

One of the most iconic locations from the famous movie series, this Tatooine map brings to life a version of the Star Wars desert planet, complete with *Millennium Falcon* and other spaceships. Including features from all the trilogies and *The Mandalorian* TV show, it's a Star Wars nerd's dream! Explore, build, and survive on Tatooine, just like you always wished you could. Our screenshots use the standard texture pack, but as the creator advises, pair it with the Conquest resource pack for best results. All it's missing is a second sun!

IMAGE: SHADOWPLAYZ95

IMAGE: SHADOWPLAYZ95

Star Wars

IMAGE: SHADOWPLAYZ95

DON'T MISS

>> **The Sarlacc Pit**, where everyone's fave Boba Fett met his end (or did he?).
>> The much-loved *Millennium Falcon*, parked in one of the bays for you to check out.
>> **Brilliant architecture** and locations familiar to any Star Wars fan.

IMAGE: SHADOWPLAYZ95

IMAGE: SHADOWPLAYZ95

COOL STUFF

>> An absolutely **huge build** that re-creates the feel of the town seen in the movies.
>> Superb **attention to detail** in the spaceships and other aspects of the build.
>> The **unmissable feeling** of being on a planet from Star Wars.

IMAGE: SHADOWPLAYZ95

Tatooine

8-Bit Parkour

CREATED BY: Moqally & Slothy
DOWNLOAD LINK: tinyurl.com/8bitparkour

Produced by two 12-year-olds, 8-Bit Parkour combines the favored Minecraft pastime of parkour with the beautiful 8-bit gaming design of the past. Jump, leap, and trick your way through a course composed of '70s, '80s, '90s, and '00s favorites, from Mario and Luigi to Pikachu, *Adventure Time*, and more! These characters come from all forms of media, and we had a great time recognizing where the beautiful pixel-art characters originated. Truly a piece of art that's both entertaining and interactive!

IMAGE: MOQALLY & SLOTHY

IMAGE: MOQALLY & SLOTHY

IMAGE: MOQALLY & SLOTHY

DON'T MISS

» **Secret barrier blocks** that can help or hinder as you try to make your way through the map.

» The appearance of a famous YouTuber's **creeper-style avatar.** Do you recognize it?

» All your **favorite characters** from cartoons and gaming!

IMAGE: MOQALLY & SLOTHY

IMAGE: MOQALLY & SLOTHY

COOL STUFF

» On top of **looking great**, it's a digestible and easy-to-complete experience.

» A fun **transition from 2D to 3D** as you progress through the levels.

» **Zero command block design,** so it should work in virtually any Java version!

IMAGE: MOQALLY & SLOTHY

IMAGE: MOQALLY & SLOTHY

133

Batman: Wa

CREATED BY: Berhan
DOWNLOAD LINK:
tinyurl.com/mc-waynemanor

Whether this is taken from the Batman games or the Batman movies is hard to tell, but one thing is certain: when someone builds Wayne Manor and the Batcave, you know there's only one superhero who lives there. This map doesn't only give you a full-size mansion to explore, but a huge Batcave beneath, where you can find the Batmobile, Bat-computer, and other recognizable elements from every iteration of Batman. Put on your best Batman skin and grapple your way down there. Finally, you are the night!

IMAGE: BERHAN

IMAGE: BERHAN

IMAGE: BERHAN

yne Manor

IMAGE: BERHAN

DON'T MISS

» There are lots and lots of hidden secrets to be found **all around the mansion**!

» A *T. rex* model, **Batmobile, giant coin**, and more found underground in the Batcave.

» **Bat-suits hidden all over the place**—or is that just Minecraft armor?

IMAGE: BERHAN

IMAGE: BERHAN

COOL STUFF

» Includes **working redstone-based elevators** for getting you to and from the Batcave.

» Locations inspired by **multiple Batman iterations,** including movies and games.

» **No shortcuts**—every room of the mansion and its caves is fully realized.

IMAGE: BERHAN

IMAGE: FA_PEW07

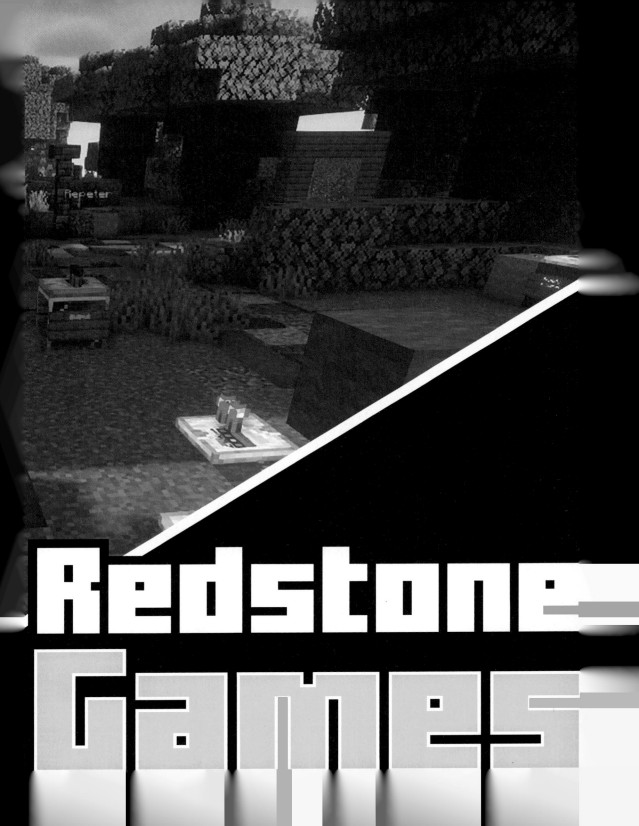

Redstone
Games

IMAGE: MATTBATWINGS

IMAGE: MATTBATWINGS

CREATED BY:
mattbatwings
DOWNLOAD LINK:
tinyurl.com/mc-redstonetetris

Tetris is one of those games that has come to almost every gaming platform, and now it's even come to Minecraft! In a way, it's surprisingly apt that two games about moving blocks around should meet in this way. Although it runs slowly, it's easy to forgive when you see the sheer size of the machine powering it. A true monument to the epic power of redstone, it's almost impossible to believe someone could have made it unless you see it working with your own eyes!

IMAGE: MATTBATWINGS

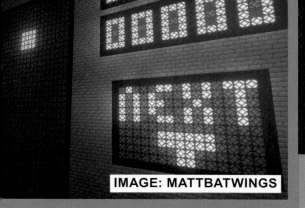

IMAGE: MATTBATWINGS

Playable Redstone Tetris

Playable Redstone Chess

IMAGE: MATTBATWINGS

IMAGE: MATTBATWINGS

IMAGE: MATTBATWINGS

CREATED BY:
mattbatwings
DOWNLOAD LINK:
tinyurl.com/mc-redstonechess

Given the complexity of the classic board game, it's hard to imagine that you could create a chess simulator using only Minecraft blocks, but that's exactly what you can find in this map. Almost more impressive than the fact that it works is that it works so well—the interface makes it so easy to play that anyone can pick it up. The only limitation is that you have to do the check/checkmate bit yourself—but let's face it, the game is already so complex that it's easy to do that small piece of work!

IMAGE: MATTBATWINGS

IMAGE: ARWENOC

CREATED BY: ArwenOC
DOWNLOAD LINK:
tinyurl.com/mc-roadrunners

Based on the popular mobile game *Crossy Road*, this game, named Road Runners, gives you a similar experience in Minecraft, using command blocks to create a mod-free, fixed-camera re-creation of the game. This is proof of what can be achieved using nothing but command blocks in Minecraft, and we think you'll be impressed whether you're a fan of *Crossy Road* or just want to see the heights of what redstone can do with the Minecraft engine.

IMAGE: ARWENOC

IMAGE: ARWENOC

IMAGE: ARWENOC

Road Runners

Redstone Explaining World

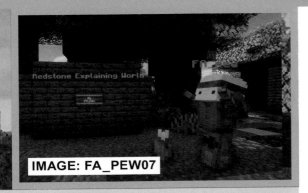

IMAGE: FA_PEW07

CREATED BY:
FA_pew07

DOWNLOAD LINK:
tinyurl.com/mc-redstoneexplainer

Learning how redstone works is a difficult part of Minecraft's gameplay, and if you've ever struggled to understand the difference between a repeater and an observer, or how to use redstone torches, this map is exactly what you need to download. Filled with simple, annotated examples of working redstone circuitry, it offers an easy way to learn how (and why) redstone can be made to help you in your own builds, no matter what your ambitions are.

IMAGE: FA_PEW07

IMAGE: FA_PEW07

IMAGE: FA_PEW07

IMAGE: THEDOGYLT

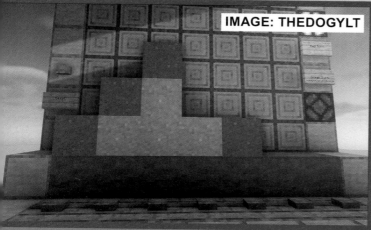

IMAGE: THEDOGYLT

CREATED BY:
TheDogYLT
DOWNLOAD LINK:
tinyurl.com/mc-connect4

We've all played a four-in-a-row game with counters and slots, but have you ever played it in Minecraft? This build uses a redstone system to release sand blocks in alternating colors, giving you and a friend a chance to play a four-in-a-row game within Minecraft. It might look complicated from the back, but up front you just have to push a button to watch the sand drop, and another when (or if) one of you wins. Impressive stuff, and it'd be a great thing to drop into any multiplayer build.

IMAGE: THEDOGYLT

IMAGE: THEDOGYLT

Four in a Row

Rock Paper Scissors

IMAGE: ALPAGUUU

CREATED BY:
Alpaguuu
DOWNLOAD LINK:
tinyurl.com/mc-rockpaperscissors

In this build you'll find a simple representation of a rock-paper-scissors game for two players, built entirely out of redstone command blocks. A simple interface hides a complex work of engineering! Hit the button and wait to see if you've outsmarted your opponent or not. One of the most simple games you can play, brought to life in an outstanding way. It's Minecraft as you've never played it, and on top of that, the build itself looks incredible thanks to the variety of colored wool blocks.

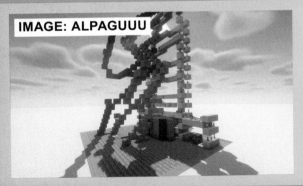

IMAGE: ALPAGUUU

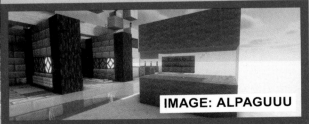

IMAGE: ALPAGUUU

IMAGE: ALPAGUUU

THE END

Published by Scholastic Inc.,
557 Broadway, New York,
NY 10012

For SBLtd
Words James Hunt
Art Editor Laura Pelham
Production Editor Phil King
Editor Simon Brew

PRINT Printed in the U.S.A. 40
ISBN: 978-1-338-85019-2
10 9 8 7 6 5 4 3 2 1   22 23 24 25 26

DISCLAIMER
Minecraft is a registered trademark of Mojang Synergies AB ("Mojang"). The screenshots and artwork shown in this publication were taken from Minecraft, a game published by Mojang, and from Microsoft XBOX websites. Game design, programming and graphics for Minecraft were authored by Notch (Markus Persson), officers, employees and/or freelancers of Mojang. This is a 100% unofficial and independent publication which is in no way licensed, authorized or endorsed by or otherwise connected in any way with Mojang or any other individuals who are authors of Minecraft.

Names, brands, and logos mentioned in this publication may be protected by trademark or other intellectual property rights of one or several legal jurisdictions. Any reference to such marks in no way implies that they are not protected under applicable law, nor is it implied that there is any commercial or other relationship between the publisher and that trademark holder.

The publisher excludes all liability for the content and services provided by any websites or other third-party publications, or games reviewed, and shall not be responsible for and does not endorse any advertising, products, or resources including those available from any third-party external resources, including websites, and we shall not be liable to any party for any information, services, or resources made available through them.

All copyrights recognized and used specifically for the purpose of criticism and review.